Romania

To Muskingum readers—
May you enjoy your trip
To Romania—

Jerry Maton

Photos printed by Applied Photographics of Battle Creek, Michigan,
with special thanks to Alan Delach

Design: Salvador Martinez Aldana

Romania

by Jerry Morton

The Jerry Lee Press
USA

This book is dedicated to the journalism students
of the University of Timisoara and the people
of Romania.

Această carte este didicată studentilor Facultăţii de
Jurnalism a Universităţii Timişoara şi poporului
român.

Introduction

I went to Romania to teach journalism and to discover its people and places.

I taught, under a Fulbright grant, at the University of Timisoara, walked the streets of the city where the revolution of 1989 began and wandered the tiny towns scattered around the countryside.

As a journalist, with notebooks and camera in hand, I recorded my impressions through pencil and film. And, in their finished form, they appear on the pages of this book.

More elusive, however, was the challenge of trapping the mood of those sidewalks and side roads, the being and image beyond words, what Romanians freely call "the soul." The feeling was everywhere, defying the traditional divisions into chapters, and titles, that define most literary volumes.

To admit that aura, or at least come close, I invite the reader to embark upon a journey of color which, appropriately, employs blue, yellow and red, the colors of the Romanian flag. This was my road map, one that may be followed directly from beginning to end or, better still, may serve as a helpful companion on a jaunt where time and direction have little meaning.

Blue is an expression of strength, of reflection and memories, even sadness. Yellow, like the sun, symbolizes brightness, hope, energy, a spiritual quality that encourages or enlightens. Red evokes passion, deep feelings of joy or sorrow, the emblems of love or of war.

These, of course, are my interpretations. You will have your own. As you travel through this book, then, may you savor your moments along its paths, among its people and, most of all, amid its colors. I hope you enjoy your journey as much as I did mine and, in the end, appreciate the many faces of Romania — and the spirit to which they belong.

Jerry Morton

Preface

Timisoara. In a city as old as this one,
it is difficult to find something new

———————□———————

The Romans were here nearly 2,000 years ago, followed over the centuries by Magyars, Turks, Austrians and Romanians, among others, all leaving cultural reminders of their own, whether in the presence of museum artifacts or in the people of today's Timisoara.

"We are a small Europe, this part of Romania," Marcel Tolcea, a University of Timisoara journalism professor, told a seminar of the Council of Europe.

"This is a secret note that allows the singing of a common song — and has done so for ages."

Perfect harmony in human affairs is rare, especially in regions that have seen many conquerors over many generations. Yet, Professor Tolcea has said it well.

This is a place that seems to grow stronger and more inviting as it changes, as Serbians cross the border 40 miles away, peasants arrive from distant villages or visitors trickle in from "The West."

But of all the changes that have ever occurred in this western Romanian town, few were as shattering as the revolution of 1989 when, if only via television, the whole world came to Timisoara.

The events of those December days belong to history now, along with the battles, agreements and other happenings that signaled the beginnings and ends of those previous eras.

The Reformed Church of Timisoara, where a series of protests by the Hungarian congregation and Romanian supporters of the Rev. Laszlo Tokes sparked a national uprising, has become a routine stop for foreign tourists.

Around the corner, trams rattle through Maria Square, past an assortment of small businesses — a pizzeria, a coffee shop with a

"Snickers" sign on the door, a German travel agency — that have sprung up in recent years.

The Romanian Orthodox Cathedral, on whose steps men, women and children were gunned down, still towers over the city center, a broad walkway with gardens and fountains in the middle and Opera Square at the opposite end.

And Alba Iulia, a street reaching into that square and without lights before the revolution, displays 1,000 tiny, white bulbs on wires above its brick pavement, brightening the doorways to the Hungarian and German theaters, machines dispensing "inghetata" (ice cream) and posters reading "Dior."

Most modifications are easily noticed, apparent to anyone who left town and returned even a short while later.

A bright facade or the coming of neon, though, is hardly remarkable in a city that has been constantly rebuilt — from Roman settlement to walled fortress to industrial center — during the course of its long existence.

For in Timisoara, the changes that matter most are the ones least easily seen.

"What the revolution was about," journalism student Pitsu Horia said, "was the explosion of the right to talk, to shout, to yell, to tell our opinion."

For journalists, then, it was about the right to tell stories, to take pictures, to gather the news and show their work to others.

"Before 1989, we were condemned to writing for drawers," Silviu Genescu, a science fiction author and foreign editor of the newspaper Timisoara, said.

"The words might be written, but no one was allowed to read them. We had to wait for better times."

Prior to the revolution, The Red Banner, an arm of the Romanian Communist Party (RCP), was Timisoara's only major newspaper.

Today, newsstands overflow with daily newspapers and with tabloids and magazines specializing in almost anything: Celebrity gossip, politics, sports, sex, crossword puzzles or murders.

The world of Romanian journalism is different now — but it always has been.

"Our press has a perfume," journalism historian Joe Farza said. "It is especially passionate and picaresque."

That tradition is exemplified by the life of Mihai Eminescu, the national poet, whose statue appears in parks and public squares.

Romanians point out, for example, that many of his poems were first published in newspapers and that Eminescu edited a paper, Timilull, in 1883.

"Days go past and days come still / All is old and all is new," a recurring line in the Eminescu poem "Gloss" declared.

There is both a journalistic truth and a poetic ring to that notion. It is a fitting statement in a country where, it seems, every sentence must have a soul.

"The Romanian news writers are really literary writers who find themselves in a newsroom and have to figure out what to do," a reporter said.

Many journalists in post-revolutionary Romania are would-be poets, essayists and novelists who, like Silviu Genescu, were trained as engineers.

Classroom instruction in journalism, the kind based upon a free press, has just begun.

And, as if reflecting Romanian society, educators seem uncertain where reporters and editors belong.

At the University of Timisoara, after all, journalism is part of the Department of Letters, Philosophy, History, Orthodox Theology, Journalism and Physical Education.

I taught in that department for a year, presenting writing and editing courses to 50 students in the English sections of the first- and second-year journalism programs.

Separated by generations, culture and journalistic outlook, it would be easy to emphasize the differences between students and teacher. In fact, it is even easier to recall the similarities that brought us together — discovered through friendship and respect, measured in those ways least easily seen.

The only visible remnants of that year are copies of In Other Words, a student publication, the first English language paper ever in Timisoara.

The newspaper was partly news and partly viewpoint, a tiny, delayed outburst of that "explosion" of years before.

In Other Words was simply a photocopied paper of from four to eight pages which sold at a university kiosk for 100 lei (about 6 cents) and covered a variety of topics.

Although I remember the students best of all, I recall, too, some of the paper's bits and pieces:

* The front page of one issue featured a story by Tina Tompea about "a restless and agitated crowd" that "fought, struggled and screamed in University Hall during a late afternoon in March."

The students, the article pointed out, were grabbing for a limited number of free books provided by a local publishing house.

"The ones who got their hands on the books wore smiles despite their creased clothing," she wrote. "Those who didn't succeed looked bitter and envious."

"That picture stresses the importance that books play in our lives."

* Carina Borchin told readers about "A Boy Named Robert," a homeless child whom she interviewed on the streets of Timisoara.

"The boy, a Gypsy, had an innocent face," she said, "and his look, usual for a child his age, could make one believe that he was happy. Behind his appearance, though, there was sadness and desperation."

After describing her conversation with Robert, she concluded: "Since life is tough for all of us, who would be so selfless as to care for 'nobody's child?' "

* Dana Schiopu remembered when, as an RCP youth brigade Pioneer before the revolution, she and thousands of other teenagers scoured streets and roads to retrieve empty vinegar bottles which, in turn, were collected by government authorities for recycling.

"Then, the students were Pioneers," she said, "and they collected bottles only for the reward of what the Communist leader called 'moral uplift.' Now they are university students, and they collect empty bottles of Coca-Cola for 200 lei (12 cents) each."

Writing about the rivalry among students in the university coffee shop, she added:

"But no one should think that this is an easy job. Now we are living in a democracy, and you cannot earn anything without a minimum of competition."

* Ramona Balutescu asked students about King Mihai (Michael), exiled since 1947 but still popular among many Romanians.

To the question "What do you think about having the King come to Romania?" a young woman replied: "I'm not interested in the King. This subject belongs to the past, at least Mihai does."

"I feel like I've been waiting for the King all of my life," a young man said. "I would be very happy if he comes back. It would be like in a fairy tale. King and Queen. And fairy tales, most of them, have a happy ending."

* Gabriel Sperneac pondered the future, saying: "In Romania, life is not very good, but this is not a reason for us to go to foreign countries."

Regarding democracy, a student commented: "Democracy will come to Romania only when people will realize that democracy is not just a way to become rich over the night."

The paper was printed in the Hi-Fi Shop, a tape and CD store located, appropriately, on Eminescu Street.

A Timisoara TV camera operator caught editor Carmen Taran and Tina pulling sheets of that first issue from a photocopy machine below a Rolling Stones poster.

The song "Games People Play" blared from above as a CD customer stared at the action, as if wondering what was so special about a stack of paper.

As always, though, Carmen was as concerned with content as with appearance.

The front page of that first edition, after all, included a "To Our Readers" commentary, in which she wrote that "some of you might not like what we will be writing about."

"But we are sure," she added, "that for those of you who will like our ideas and our work, this English newspaper will seem like a password for opening secret doors into the unknown which will not be a mystery for you any more."

Students liked the paper well enough to purchase all 300 copies within three days, prompting a staff writer to look well beyond the next deadline.

"We should return in 10 years to see how far this paper has come," Sorin Stan said. "Someone may put a plaque on the Hi-Fi shop saying 'In this building, on this site' and so forth."

I am not certain what will be remembered in 10 years, and the Hi-Fi shop, as yet, is without an historical marker.

What matters to me is that the students added their voice, however slight, to those other voices that arose following the revolution.

"These are the children of yesterday," a professor had told me, referring to the 1990s generation of Romanian college students. "They will not be called upon to do great things."

In a nation where expression was repressed for so long, and where today's university students grew up under the old ways, there may be some truth to that observation.

But that teacher did not know the students I knew, at least the ones eager for the challenges of a new Romania.

In the rest of this book you will find stories and pictures that I compiled on short journeys during my stay in Timisoara.

They were gathered with a sense mission and a sense of joy, elements that I hope are reflected on the following pages.

As the years go by, however, Carmen, Tina, Sorin and their colleagues will offer other stories of Romanian life as only they can tell them, with special insights that only they can reveal.

So as I filled this book with my views and adventures, I felt I must introduce you, if only briefly, to theirs.

For I know that whatever they eventually do and say is certain to contribute something new — even in a city, and a country, as old as this one.

Where gas pumps
meet the clover

Dumbravita. Cira and Vioara Petrovici married young

———————□———————

"We were 15 and 18," he said, remembering how they had begun their lives together more than 60 years before.

" Yes," she said, seeking to clarify that statement, "but almost 16 and 19."

Whatever the ages, both agree that that was a long time back, years after their families had brought their children in rented wagons from the same Serbian village to Dumbravita where Cira and Vioara met and married.

And while the Petrovicis have remained in the same town for six decades that does not mean they have stayed in the same place.

For though they have not moved to the city, the city — Timisoara — has moved to them.

" The village is barely a village anymore," he said. "I once lived at the end. Now we live in the middle."

That is a way of describing Dumbravita's transition, not quite accomplished, from rural village to Timisoara suburb, a trend which touches small places throughout the country as prosperity, whatever its speed, comes to Romania.

It is a change best seen on the edges of Timisoara, the flat, open spaces where old and new converge.

The last stop on the Timisoara bus line offers such a setting, circled, as it is, by apartment buildings with the trees of Dumbravita in sight three miles down the busy highway.

The hike to the village took me along the shoulder, past clover fields where a stone cross, guarded by a sheep dog, stood close to the road.

In those fields, a chestnut horse grazed as workers wearing red bandannas piled the clover into a wooden wagon.

They gathered the harvest with hand sickles, cut the plants in an even row, then returned to start over.

If the scene, an age-old legacy with a modern backdrop, had the aura of a painting, the realities, for the workers, were much more pressing.

For across the fields, other laborers, in coveralls and baseball caps, armed with cement blocks and steel beams, were building a service station.

A sign, "4 Star Texaco," firmly planted next to a rut that will one day become a driveway, had the look of a flag laying claim to the land.

The ruts extended to the road, and empty holes awaited the arrival of gas pumps.

On the far end of the clover fields, a billboard said something else:

" Banatul" — a development that will bring 60 houses and 105 apartments and offices to those fields.

" For You," the advertisement read, inviting customers to visit the brick, single-story office beside the billboard.

The entrance to Dumbravita, though, was more welcoming. The trees almost formed an arch over the road, and the peaceful, side streets were coated with crushed stones of many colors.

The Petrovicis live on one of those side streets in a house where work seldom ceases, though the routine differs from what it used to be.

As a younger man, Cira Petrovici had passed the clover fields each day on a bicycle to and from his job in a Timisoara wool factory.

Now he stays at home, tending to his cherry trees and grape arbor.

"This is where I work these days," he said. "It is safer than traveling on the road. No? "

While he spoke, Vioara Petrovici boiled cherries in an iron kettle in a brick shed, the fire fueled by cornstalks, wisps of smoke wafting over the wet, green trees and vines on the rainy afternoon.

Then Cira, dressed in blue sweater and gray hat, propped a ladder against the trees, climbed to pick a handful of cherries and invited me to do the same.

Later, we sat on a patio by the garden, a bowl of cherries, a plate of tomatoes and onions, and mint tea by our side.

It was a pleasant day in the suburban village, a day that flowed with ease for three people who sought fleeting glimpses into other worlds.

I could only wonder what Dumbravita looked like when the clover fields almost touched the Petrovici doorsteps or the days the horses and wagons arrived from Serbia.

The Petrovicis were wondering, too, about what they might learn from the first American they had ever met, about whether, for starters, the people in the United States resemble the characters on "Dallas."

The program had been the most popular television show for years, so popular, in fact, that late Tuesday and Saturday nights were said to be the only times for Romanians to buy gasoline without having to wait in line.

"I like to watch Dallas," he said, "but I liked the first part a bit better than the last."

"I'll miss it when it's over, but something else will come along."

Before I left Dumbravita, we watched a World Cup preview, one that promised "goals to take your breath away," laughing when none of them did.

And when it was time to leave, as the twilight neared, Vioara Petrovici handed me a jar of cherries and a loaf of freshly-baked bread.

I might have caught a bus from Dumbravita but decided to wait until I reached the town, giving me one more opportunity to pass through the clover fields.

As I did, all was quiet, workers and wagon gone, a neat edge revealing where the laborers had left off and would one day begin again.

The Timisoara skyline, dominated by the Romanian Orthodox Cathedral, was in view, and, with each step, the city inched closer, as it always seems to do.

Windows and an Easter walk

Oravita. When twilight comes to Oravita,
the windows come alive

———————□———————

They fill with people, or fill with gold, and flavor a walk down Andrei Saguna Street.

A woman with a floral scarf leans out of a brown, stucco house, a boy peeks at passers-by, and windows still empty are left to glisten in the sun.

Though darkness will soon arrive, it will not stay for long. Not on this night, this Easter eve, a time of prayer, of color and of light.

I walk as far as an outdoor cafe promoting large Pepsi ("Pepsi En Gros") across from a movie theater showing "Evadatul" ("The Fugitive") starring Harrison Ford and return to the home of Corneliu and Aurelia Jumanca where I am spending the weekend.

Earlier, I had hiked the green hills above Oravita, overlooking the Serbian border, with son Virgil Jumanca, through pastures and beside an abandoned copper mine, near places where legends were born.

A century-old tale tells of a teacher turned outlaw who stole from wealthy landowners and retreated to the mountains. Eventually he was caught and hanged, but his gold, the legend goes, remains stashed in a cave.

The story of the Jumanca household is told in more visible ways: In wedding photos, in a picture of Corneliu in an Army uniform, and in a collection of stamps whose images —King Mihai, Lenin, the Hammer and Sickle — offer a modern history of one country and, like the U.S. stamps depicting the Astronauts, a brief insight into others.

Corneliu Jumanca saw battle on two fronts in World War II, at Stalingrad and, in the closing days, in Czechoslovakia.

After his farm was seized in 1947, he worked a small parcel and taught at an Oravita elementary school.

Today his barnyard is home to pigs, chickens and geese, and tomorrow the courtyard will be shaded by overhanging grapevines when Easter dinner is served in mid-afternoon.

Later, at midnight , I join Virgil and Rodica Jumanca and their teen-age children, Octavia and Mircea, in greeting the Orthodox Easter.

The sky in black, the air bracing as we walk to the 150-year-old St. Elijah Church where worshipers have gathered on the sidewalk in front.

A priest appears, and lights flicker, a couple at first, then many more as candles pass among the congregation.

The line begins to move, winding its way along Andrei Seguna, the marchers chanting or talking or smiling at friends who celebrate from sidewalks or from houses.

The tradition is being followed in cities and towns throughout Romania, an ancient rite with a splendor untarnished by symbols of changing times.

Older women wear black scarves and dark dresses while many of the younger sport blue jeans and sweatshirts or, in one instance, a fluorescent Nike jacket.

At the front, the flag of St. George bobs above the crowd, next to a brown cross, carried by a man in a black suit keeping pace behind the priest. And, from within the parade, the banner mingles with signs in store windows touting Marlboro cigarettes, the national lottery (Loto Prono) and the Romanian soccer team.

Children in trees, faces illuminated by the glow from a stack of tires set ablaze on the river bank, wave to the passing marchers.

The windows, too, are once again alive, twinkling with orange bulbs or candle flames and decorated with flowers or with the pictures of the families inside.

The procession continues by the motorina (service station), the furniture store, the clock repair shop and the Jumanca home, where a cross and candle grace a window.

We leave the march before its completion, as others are starting to do.

In the kitchen, Aurelia Jumanca has prepared a midnight snack, though the offering is much larger than that.

Slices of fresh bacon and sausage, chunks of goat's cheese and sections of hard-boiled eggs decorate brightly-colored plates on a cement table in the middle of the room, and a bucket of cool water rests near the doorway.

At the table, the Jumancas talk about their Saturday, about the procession, about their plans for Easter, their quiet tones blending with the soft background of Serbian folk songs on the radio.

The music fades as I walk to the parlor where I will sleep, down a long hallway, past a sketch of Mihai Eminescu, and walls adorned with floral tapestries.

Through the curtains, I notice that the streets are deserted, the windows dark.

And on a day that has offered much on Andrei Seguna, this time is the most memorable of all, this time between an Easter welcome bound to be remembered and an Easter sunrise still to come.

Haycarts after the rain

Cilnic. Rainbows seldom finish second

———————————□———————————

And when they do, the journey was special, indeed.

I felt that way after roaming the gentle hills near Sibiu through Girbova, Cilnic and Cut by train, bus and foot — and another means of travel that belonged to others.

These are old and tranquil places, dating to Roman times, where one might find a fortress or a Gothic church at the end of a narrow, winding street.

On the road from Girbova, though, the sky was the top attraction, dark and crossed by lightning as the bus rolled into Cilnic's main square. Then, as I stepped down, the rain, accompanied by blasts of thunder, began to fall, quickly turning dust to mud and prompting me to seek shelter.

The destination was a coffee house, a large, unlighted room with steel tables and tall windows where journalist Gogot Constantin and I joined a dozen young customers in waiting out the storm.

Although coffee was in greatest demand, the tables held other enticements: Milky Way bars, Sylvester Stallone posters and World Wrestling Federation trading cards.

Outdoors, there would be more, like the school with a courtyard mural, the Catholic church with its lofty spire and other remnants of a once-dominant German community.

But as the scenes unfolded, I would best remember the haycarts and how they drifted through the streets on what had become a clear and cool afternoon.

The first appeared shortly after I left the coffee house — a wagon stacked with hay, pulled by a black horse and guided by a woman, holding a stick, who walked alongside.

Although such wagons are common on the streets and roads of rural Romania, they were eye-catching to me, perhaps because they command attention, as a slowly-moving building would do.

Or because they belong to another era.

Or because they know exactly where they belong, traveling, as they do, with a sense of grace, fitting a village like words fitting nicely into a poem.

"Haycarts make their way along the old road where wild cherry trees putting their heads together could be keeping count as the carts pass," Romanian poet Otilia Cazimir wrote.

And if wooden utility poles outnumbered cherry trees on the thoroughfares of Cilnic, counting haycarts still seemed a worthy pastime on an August day in a Transylvania town.

When another passed by, I decided to follow, snapping pictures of a boy, dog under his arm, sitting low and sideways in the back seat, beneath the hay pile and right between the wheels.

Then I ran to take a closer look, overtaking the wagon at the edge of the village.

The driver, a woman in a black coat and wearing a wide-brimmed hat, pulled the reins on the dapple-gray horse and, when all was still, chatted before moving on.

She told us she was headed home, to a farm two miles away, and that the passengers — a boy at her side and the one in back — were grandsons.

The view was a rare one — the woman conversing, the boy staring down, blue sky in back, gold hay in front — and nearly the last I would see in Cilnic.

For Cut was next, five miles down a country road but shorter for us, perhaps, with a walk across open field.

The hike was enjoyable, even through wet weeds and patches of burrs, and, toward the middle, came a bonus: a rainbow over the slopes beyond Cilnic.

On most days, a rainbow, having draped its arc of color over a previously threatening sky, would be the instant best remembered.

But this late afternoon belonged to the wagons, the ones in Cilnic and still another up ahead.

"All that rain has made the hay sneeze," Barbu Fundoianu wrote.

"Now the carts on which it lies mowed have crushed the pebbles of light and the evening is fresh."

The poet had captured the flavor of the moment, though this cart, on a trail through a cornfield, gave the pastoral scene yet another slant with a driver who wore a New York Yankees cap.

The young man and his father, who rode in back, were taking the short cut, too, having gathered the hay near Cut and returning to their farm on the other side of Cilnic.

"This is good for us," the man said, as if speaking of both the rain and the hay as he stood proudly beside his cart.

"We worked hard, and tomorrow we will work some more."

The sound of hoof beats and wheels faded as we continued on toward Cut, now an array of dwellings on a hillside.

After we scampered up an embankment and crossed a paved road, we arrived at the railroad station and checked the schedule on the blackboard.

The train was still a couple minutes away when we reached the concrete sweep near the ticket window.

The depot itself was a tiny booth in the back of a house where the railroad business had interrupted the business of boiling potatoes as a boy sat at a dinner table and ducks blocked the doorway.

When the train arrived, it quickly left, on toward Sibiu through villages reduced to dimly-lighted signs in the fast-rushing darkness.

And on a day that had offered a surprise with almost every step, there was, at last, little to see.

For by now, the haycarts were gone from sight as well, having reached their havens far along the old roads where wild cherry trees — and captivated travelers — keep count.

A town of tiny miracles

Parta. You can't hear history in Parta

———————□———————

Sometimes it only seems that way.

Especially beyond the fence dressed by little, blue wildflowers in the yard of the Orthodox Church where a cross and marker honor choir members killed in World War I.

To pause beside the monument as voices fill the sanctuary during Sunday mass is to feel, for a moment, the bond between the singers inside and the "two basses" and "two tenors" written in stone, long silent but long remembered.

When mass is over, the worshipers pass the memorial to greet the Rev. Petgu Ioan, the priest who serves the Romanian church and the Serbian church across the street and whose duties for this Sunday are not finished.

Young and old chat a while, then pause when they see a visitor with a camera.

A grandmother insists on a picture and, granddaughter at her side, smiles while a man in a wool cap and overcoat waits patiently by the gate where the priest had stood moments before.

Rev. Petgu, meanwhile, has returned inside where people sit on folding chairs and wooden benches in the small church, and a husband, wife and infant daughter are the center of attention.

As the priest prepares to perform the baptismal ritual he does so in a shiny gold and yellow robe and holds a silver cross.

The young man, bearing a candle, seems a bit bewildered, but his wife, dressed in black with a silver-threaded jacket, calmly holds the girl with one hand as Rev. Petgu chants, and an old man with thick glasses and a crackly voice responds.

The priest cuts three locks of hair and sprinkles feet and hands with oil and water while the girl stares at the ceiling.

Bulbs symmetrically arranged in a chandelier light the sanctuary where banners with emblems depicting biblical miracles drape the walls. The largest celebrates the recovery of Lazarus through the figure of a man carrying a large bed.

The baptism, like the choir, represents both continuity and a beginning, symbols important within the community, as well as within the church.

For as I cross the main street, a broad and rutted roadway best fit for horses or tractors, particularly after a spring rain, I am followed by three children who make me feel as if I have started a parade.

The two girls smile, wave and head in the opposite direction after I snap their pictures. But the boy, Danny, about 10, hangs around, posing in the middle of the street, hand on hip and knit cap tightly on his head, then showing how much English he knows by talking about basketball player Michael Jordan.

He is standing alone, the road and the overcast sky behind him, against a line of cherry trees and plum trees and a string of houses, stucco dwellings in earth colors of ocher and pale green.

The village population is about 600, less than half of what it once was, and, with little work at home and a big city — Timisoara — 15 miles away, it is likely that the next generation, as the present one, will seek to leave Parta.

But for those who have stayed, even through the hardest of times, there are many stories to tell.

Radu Milovan, whose father was jailed after World War II for opposing farm collectivization, was sent to prison for speaking out against the government.

Today, his family has reclaimed a fraction of its lost acreage and, from a house on the wide street, strives to secure a link between past and present.

"Before the revolution," he said, "it was as if the past had been erased."

"Our memories were those our leaders allowed us to have."

In Romanian villages, though, memories are not so easily disposed of, not in the Milovan home where a wedding album and a blouse stitched by a grandmother long ago —with quality cotton, black-thread embroidery and loving care— turn a living room into a family shrine.

History is preserved, too, in the words of Radu Milovan, whose grandfather founded the church choir in 1893, and in the picture of King Mihai hanging on the salmon-colored wall of the kitchen.

For the Milovans, as well as for other villagers, such reminders are not just matters of nostalgia but of tradition, of transmission, of something needed to live on.

In the back, meanwhile, there is room for two horses, two cows, some pigs, a dozen fat geese and a strutting turkey which shows its feathers. The horses, Milovan said, are retained out of respect and affection, but the other animals mean another start, another chance to rebuild.

As he speaks, he does so with pride and promise, items not easily apparent on a cloudy day in this village.

Even a few more tractors and a few more businesses would bring "good success" to the town, he said.

For now, he talks of the new coffee house at the corner, a renewed interest in painting fences and the presence of a doctor who lives on the next street.

Tiny miracles — and something more.

For as I am about to leave, Milovan shows off his electrified corn wheel, a machine which means he will no longer have to grind the animal feed by hand.

The wheel makes a whirring noise, not loud enough to startle the geese — but another sound worth hearing on a quiet day in Parta.

Snapshots near a dark station

Maureni. They were just kids

———————□———————

A little boy and his two sisters.

And I met them only briefly on a dark and rainy afternoon while waiting for a train after a hike through the countryside.

But I remember them more than anything else from that day, and I wonder if they remember the visitor who took their picture.

I saw the boy as I crossed the double tracks and walked toward the Maureni station, a brick depot with red roof that, except for the name on top, might have stood in Voiteg or Forotic or Surduc Banat or any other farm town on the line south of Timisoara.

I bought my ticket, a tiny piece of green cardboard, for 35 cents, from the agent posted in the cramped compartment by the door. The hallway was dim, catching little light from the bulb inside the ticket booth, and, by now, the sky had darkened, too.

Earlier in the day, I had arrived at Gataia, five miles away, and had taken side roads through farmfields and sheep country, as well as Highway 58B, all under a clear sky and with a gentle breeze.

Now, the wind was whipping the clothesline behind the house across from the station as a woman pulled shirts and blankets into her arms.

And, on my side of the rails, dust was swirling near the orange, stucco house next to the track, perhaps a former station, where two girls had appeared.

They joined the boy in the road in front and stared at me as I stood on the platform, waiting for a train that was 15 minutes away.

I walked toward the children, and, within moments, they began running my way, finally stopping and grabbing my arms as if to see what the stranger was made of.

The boy, round-eyed, curley-haired and wearing a gray T-shirt over red-striped pajama bottoms, followed my "Hello" with one of his own, then continued to repeat everything I said.

One of the girls, whose brown hair hid brass earrings, pointed to her shiny tennis shoes, almost covered by her blue-and-white checkered dress, and placed one next to my mine, a Transylvania brand, now scruffy, which I had purchased in Timisoara. Then she laughed, as if convinced she had gotten the better deal.

The other girl merely giggled, perhaps wondering who was the sillier, her sister and her brother or the traveler who had wandered into their lives.

This was one of those happy surprises that makes a journey worth recalling, coming unexpectedly, when a trip is almost over.

For the children had emerged as luminous figures against the somber background, fluttering spirits in a playground of steel and concrete.

Or, more simply, they were kids who laughed and shouted as if cheering life itself, a celebration worth watching, whatever the time and place.

I reached for my camera, which hung around my neck, and went to one knee, angling for a perfect photo of the children standing close together.

With that, they crouched, too, then sat on the edge of a wagon to create an even better picture.

After a minute, though, the boy ran home and, almost as quickly, his sisters followed.

With the beginning of the rain, I returned to the station and joined two women in waiting for the train.

The rain beat hard against the door windows and through a square where the glass was missing.

A long bench rested in the hall, but, like the others, I decided to stand. We all preferred the view of rain against the window over the drab, green wall facing the bench.

As I waited, the door swung wide open, and the boy reappeared, slightly out of breath, and a little soggy from his dash through the rain.

I noticed something different but could not tell what it was.

Then I spotted his cheeks, caked with rouge, in anticipation of another photo.

I obliged, pointing at the open window from the outside, where I was partially protected by an overhang, and trying to capture my subject as he peeked through.

I pulled my notebook from my shirt pocket and was about to ask the boy to write his name.

But before I could, other passengers had left for the platform, preparing for the arrival of the train, now a faint beam breaking the gloom of the storm.

And then he disappeared again, this time behind a house gate where a woman waved at me as the train approached.

By now, the ticket seller had reached the tracks, too, equipped with a red and green paddle that,with the raising of his arm, would eventually send the train on its way.

While trains stop often in Maureni, they do not stop for long.

I had barely scaled the first step, in fact, when the train began to move.

Turning around, I saw the orange, stucco house, the train coming so close I almost felt I could touch the walls.

A light, framed by window curtains, flashed by and, in the yard, a gray horse stood at a watering trough.

I did not see the children again. Their faces would next appear to me only in black and white pictures.

But I thought of them on the trip to Timisoara, recalling how vibrant and alive they were and how I hoped they would stay that way for a long, long time.

As I said, they were just kids—but sometimes, half a world away from that house near the station, I think of them still.

blue

blue

38

Summer steps and
hidden places

Singeorge. If you enjoy walking a country road, the
name of the country does not really matter

The signs may read "Hodunk," "Shultz," or "Ceresco," as they do
in my part of Michigan, or "Birda," "Manastire," or "Singeorge," as
they do in western Romania.

But with a road ahead, and time on your side, a summer day speaks
a common language, whatever the point on the globe.

And on a bright, July morning when a trip might start at any point,
mine began on another road — a railroad — in a place called Birda.

I had known Birda, from earlier trips farther south, as merely a
depot and a name.

This time it did not take long to learn something more, that the
most direct way to town is a mile away down a path in a cornfield,
with a flock of geese at route's end.

When I reached the center, the town was barely awake, but that
did not dampen the journey.

For little places give little pleasures, and Birda, even during a short
visit, offered its share:

Fresh bread sold from a sidewalk table; a small boy smiling as he
lifted a shutter and watched me pass by; and a white horse grazing
between hay stacks as a farmer hitched his wagon.

The destinations, after all, were really the roads themselves and
the surprises they might offer, winding, as they did, from village to
village, often disappearing from the map.

Romania, a country slightly larger than Oregon, in fact, has more
than 13,000 villages, many of which are tucked into mountains or
appear at the end of roads known only to the nearest neighbors.

On the flat lands near Birda, though, the towns are not easy to hide.

During the three-mile trek down a dirt trail to Manastire, for example, Birda remained in view, and, about halfway, I stopped to look at both: Birda with its rows of red roofs and trees and the Orthodox church jutting above it all and Manastire, a hamlet beside a sluggish, meandering stream arched by a stone bridge.

I did not cross the bridge, pausing, instead, to watch shepherd boys spread a blanket in a field and observe their sheep under the noonday sun.

And I looked at a rusted, metal arrow pointing to "Singeorge," uncharted territory, a place that was not supposed to be.

My map had not listed Singeorge, about the size of Manastire, but it was real to the tractor, horses and wagons that passed me on the dusty stretch into town.

The community itself had less activity, silent at midday, except for a folk song on a cafe juke box and the thud created by four boys kicking a soccer ball down the street.

I took a picture of the young athletes as they posed, kneeling, under a tree, arms around shoulders, ball in the middle, a scaled-down version of the Romanian World Cup team poster.

Later, I saw three more children —Petronella, Florin and Nicu— standing under the "Singeorge" limits sign, as if ready to escort me out of town.

The sign showed black lettering on a white background with a red diagonal through the name.

And while that was the end of Singeorge, it did not complete my day.

For the children headed for a clump of trees and a large pond where cows had gathered to keep cool.

Petronella and Florin arrived first, wading in, edging toward the cows, then kicking in all directions.

Nicu, meanwhile, was taking his time. He was not so concerned with making a splash as with catching a fish.

So he tied a thread to the end of a long stick, dipped it into the water and began to wait.

This was a scene with a universal touch — kids, cows, a fishing pole, a pond — even if a little old-fashioned, even if so far from home.

And it reminded me how much, and how little, I might see during other moments of wandering on other cloudless days.

For, at this pace, three villages each day, it would take nearly a century and a half of summers to touch all the tiny places in Romania.

All the more reason, then, to cherish both the setting and the afternoon, and simply being in a country where I could keep on walking, and could even get lost, without ever losing my way.

Road show on a Sunday

Faget. The clarinet player glanced at the poster of "Madalina Sultana," sipped his tea and wondered if he could be doing better

---

"If we played here, we might make money, have fun," he said, looking to his friend for encouragement.

"Do not be so certain," his colleague replied from across the table.

"Remember: This is Lugoj, not Las Vegas."

The presence of the Banatul Professional Ensemble of Timisoara, in the dining room of the Triol Hotel, in fact, was hardly a command performance but a rest stop on the way to somewhere else.

And the small stage in the corner, on a Sunday morning and without the dancer Sultana, lacked the glitz and dazzle of what a Triol sign had promoted as the "Superb Atmosphere" of the night before.

Instead, the cafe in Lugoj was a place for the 20-piece orchestra to pause halfway between Timisoara and a town where its style and purpose would be better accepted — Faget, site of the Spring Festival Competition.

The bus ride through the green fields of western Romania was smooth, on time and comfortable enough even for the passengers who sat on instrument cases in the aisle.

The trip was uneventful, too, except for talk about the saxophone player up front who had married the previous day.

At Faget, the orchestra would accompany visiting performers who danced and sang in the community's Cultural House.

"This is to keep our popular Romanian music in the minds of the people," festival director Ion Oltean said of the program, which he hoped would become an annual event.

"We are a little piece in the world, but little pieces are important."

43

Oltean spoke from his desk in a room off the theater lobby, a map of Romania on the wall behind him, a red accordian resting next to the door.

The Cultural House itself resembled a U.S. movie theater of yesteryear, the kind which showed "shoot 'em up" Westerns and other "B" films on Saturday afternoons.

The wavy floor boards creaked as the audience filled rows of wooden seats, and streams of sunlight found spaces where drapes did not quite cover the windows.

But in ways that mattered, the Cultural House almost sparkled, rekindling, as it did, a spirit that had weathered even the bleakest of times.

As the musicians took their seats on stage, Oltean introduced the judges who would rate the contestants.

And when the show began, the reaction to the scoring resembled that of a gymnastics meet with the audience providing evaluations of its own.

A thin, young man in high, black boots, white pants and red blouse, who had sung about moonlight in the mountains, winced as the judges announced "fives" and "sixes" — on a 10-point scale — even as the listeners jeered and whistled their disapproval.

Then, when a woman with a booming voice vocalized about lost love, the man in front of me offered a personal opinion.

"She is trying to call the sheep home," he said. "We are here for the singing."

Mostly, though, the audience liked what it saw and heard.

The ensemble was fulfilling its mission, too, adjusting its sound and pace to the manner and volume of the players who wove their own "little pieces" of popular music into a large and colorful fabric in the Cultural House of Faget.

When intermission arrived, I discovered, as well, that the cultural festival had overflowed into the theater's backyard, maybe even further.

For a busload of dancers from Jimbolia had gathered behind the Cultural House, waiting for their turn to go on. Clad in vivid costumes in a rainbow of colors, they looked like performers in a country festival of a century ago.

In reality, they were young people on the verge of entering the 21st century and doing what they might be expected to do — laugh, mug for my camera and, later, demand their friends to quiet down as they climbed the back stairway toward center stage.

When the last dancer had disappeared into the theater, I stayed on the streets of Faget to relish a festival of another kind.

Those streets were stages, too, where men played checkers, children simply played, and an old woman shared a bench with a white cat.

I would spend two hours, in fact, walking the narrow streets and watching the people of Faget, aware, too, that many were watching me.

For a while, I joined a couple who had pointed to an empty chair in the shade beside their house.

Speaking different languages, there was not too much to talk about — but that was not important.

It was enough just to sit with Nicolaie and Anna Buicar as dusk approached on Celmore Street, even though the Buicars would give me something more.

For when I left, I did so with a loaf of bread, a chunk of pork and a half dozen onions wrapped in white paper and tied with a string.

On other days, those souvenirs might soon disappear, especially when shared with fellow passengers on the return to Timisoara.

Now, though, another matter would come first, a dinner in the Cultural House.

As the final contestants were appearing on stage downstairs, tables were being prepared upstairs, along with the soups, vegetables, meats and pastries that would reward festival organizers and the performers at the end of a long and successful show.

The tables were set beneath a ceiling painted blue with gold stars. And after the guests entered the dining hall, each stood by a chair, as if awaiting the appearance of a celebrity.

Ion Oltean was there, along with the mayor of Faget.

But the scene would not be complete until the arrival of the real stars of the day, the members of the Banatul Professional Ensemble of Timisoara, who entered the room in single file behind director Radu Vincu.

As they appeared, the other guests clapped their hands and remained standing until orchestra members had been seated.

The musicians were being awarded their prize, in the unanimous judgment of all who had heard them play.

And if this was hardly Las Vegas, or even Lugoj, no one seemed to mind.

For on a special Sunday before an audience that cared, the sound of applause was all the ensemble had really needed.

48

Bats, rocks and
heavenly spaces

Romanesti. Romanian rock concerts have plenty
of rocks — at least the ones in Pestera Romanesti

———————□———————

That is where music and a couple hundred hikers joined the cave's
usual inhabitants — perhaps 1,000 bats — on a Sunday afternoon in
mid-October for an event that owes its life to an explorers' club and
its style to a revolution.

Posters on walls and telephone poles had promoted the "concert
de muzica electronica" for weeks, not mentioning that the walk
required to reach the concert hall lends as much intrigue, adventure
and tradition to the day as the music.

My journey began in the Gara De Nord railroad station where
Ramona Balutescu, a university sophomore and a reporter for the
newspaper Timisoara, and Adrian, an editor, tickets in hand, met me
in a line that snaked its way to a dimly-lighted window with gray
curtains where a woman was dispensing small, tan "biletes."

"Now we are ready for a day of riding," Ramona said, "but mostly
of walking."

The hiking, though, would come later. For now, we settled in for
a three-hour trip to the village of Faget, an excursion aboard five
worn-out, blue cars that rattled and swayed past the outskirts of
Timisoara.

But set against a golden, October morning, and with a cargo of
college students prepared to enjoy the day, the train met its task,
carrying passengers through fields adorned with cornstalks and
wooden crosses, past stations named "Cosava" and "Clicova" and
beside roads where the diesel engine and cars outraced horse-drawn
wagons.

At Faget, 200 concert goers embarked upon a mile walk to the bus station, startling ducks and chickens enroute but otherwise causing little stir in a place that had not yet come alive.

Romanesti, a community of about 400, was not fully awake either when the students arrived in four busloads. Some villagers seemed curious, but one woman stood in the middle of the road and shared a basket of apples with the visitors.

The rest of the trip, as Ramona had suggested, would be on foot, up a hill that, within a half-hour, looked more like a mountain. An 18th century Romanian Orthodox Church, its dome visible above the trees, appeared on one side and, further on, pointed, wooden fences lined the route.

And finally, Romanesti became a scattering of houses in a green and yellow valley, a vista that included a larger cluster that was Faget.

The path to the cave was muddy in spots, explaining a squishing sound as the invaders in Pro Sport, Converse, Activ and Adidas tennis shoes met the Romanian hillside.

"In the newspaper, we wrote this as a 45-minute trip," Adrian said, noting that the walk had already taken an hour. "Our stories are not always true."

To gear up for the final assault, or only to enjoy the view, many walkers pulled bread and cheese from their packs, content to sit by the trail as others overtook them.

Near the top, even younger climbers, grade-school children with an adult leader, watched as we went by, a girl in a Yamaha shirt pointing emphatically to the left as if directing traffic.

"The kids are laughing," Ramona said. "They are afraid we will be lost without their help."

The road did twist and turn, taking us to a clearing where we could hear the jingle of sheeps' bells, if not see the sheep, and leading to a shady spot that was the entrance to Pestera (Cave) Romanesti.

With the concert 20 minutes away, the hikers stood outside behind a rope, staring into the darkness for a possible glimpse at what was ahead, waiting for someone to collect the 200 lei (12 cents) admission.

Ramona and Adrian, meanwhile, had pushed toward the front, showing press badges and trying to help me pass beyond the rope without one.

"Michigan," I heard Adrian say, as he discussed the matter with a member of the Speotimis Cave Explorers Club, who wore a miner's cap with lighted candle.

With that, the man approached, shook hands and offered an official look at Pestera Romanesti.

"Michigan," I said, smiling, saying the magic word once again, just to be sure.

As we walked on, the concert area, with its synthesizer, cords and wires, became clear beneath the glare of white lights strung amid the rocks.

But behind the apparatus, there was more cave to see, a point Marcel, our guide, made clear as he directed us on a slippery tour among the crags and crevices. At the back wall, about 50 yards from the "stage," he paused and pointed his flashlight toward the ceiling.

The first known residents of the cave were members of the Cucuteni culture who had lived there nearly 10,000 years before. But while human inhabitants had disappeared, others remained.

"Since you are journalists, I have one sensational news," Marcel said, as if letting me in on a secret. "We have bats."

"Once we had 10,000, even more. Too many visitors for too many years have made them go. Now maybe 1,000."

The possibility of bats seemed natural enough, though I had never associated them with electronic music. But, for whatever reason, they were keeping to themselves.

"More sensational news," Marcel added, as he abandoned the search and helped guide me through a gap between large boulders.

"I was married here in this place. You see that it serves many purposes. All good ones, I think."

The Speotimis Club had organized the first cave concert in 1984, beginning with a symphony orchestra and moving forward, each October, with classical soloists or a chamber ensemble.

"Young people, everyone, could see our beautiful sights, and for not much money," Marcel said, "and they could hear a lovely sound."

Then, following the revolution, club members sensed what Marcel called "a profound change in our social life" and altered the program at Pestera Romanesti.

In 1990, for example, the show featured the Bega Blues Band, followed the next autumn by the rock group Survival. A trio of musicians would make up today's concert, or so the program said.

When I returned to the center of the cavern, Ramona was interviewing a young man with blue jeans, a demin jacket and an LA Kings cap, while a second performer, clad in an orange jacket, baggy trousers, a blue, neck scarf and gray, stocking cap, was twanging an electric guitar.

"Our colleague will not be here today," Adam Budritzan was saying, "but the noise will still be loud. For me, please be patient. I have never been inside a cave before."

The audience, though, was showing its patience even before Adam and his partner. Gabi Bucataru, struck the first note. While we took our walk, the hikers had entered the cavern and were standing quietly behind piles of stones, with candles sticking from the top, the dividing line between musicians and audience.

Many stood with hands in pockets, as the temperature hovered around 40 degrees, and gazed at the instruments, for them a greater attraction than the brown, gold and red hues of the cavern walls, even as the program had lagged a half-hour with no beginning in sight.

If earlier visitors had viewed the work of the Cucutenis — pottery and stone axes with handles — with awe during the Neolithic Age, the current guests were equally amazed by more recent signs of progress: An ASI computer, an Ultimate speaker and a sound machine called the "Tempo 120."

As for me, I was seated with Ramona in the press section, a thin slice of blue foam on sharp and lumpy rocks, between the viewers and musicians, waiting for the show to begin.

The program did start with a rendition of "Heavenly Spaces," a series of chords, of varying amplification, on guitar and keyboard that at least filled the quiet spaces of Pestera Romanesti.

The duo stood sideways to the crowd, Gabi striking his strings while looking at Adam for direction, and Adam with eyes glued to the ASI screen as his hand moved the "mouse" that gave proper voice to the computer-assisted music.

"You can have great influence on this performance," Adrian said, noticing a thick, orange cord, the computer's source of life, near my foot. "Be careful — or do not be."

But before I could answer, a sputtering sound emerged from a wire near the keyboard, a distraction that caused a fox terrier in a gray sweater to bark twice, giving the listeners their first laugh of the day.

"Intermission," Adam said, as he, Gabi and a woman in a black, leather skirt and orange beret checked the screen and wires.

"The bats, I expect them to drop," Ramona said, reviewing what she had heard so far, "but people are just happy to be in the cave, to look at the rocks. I cannot be critical."

I had enjoyed the performance, too, though, like Ramona and Adrian, I thought it was time to leave Pestera Romanesti without seeming ungrateful to our hosts. That might not come easy after sitting on a rock pile for two hours, but, with a smile, a wave, a slide and a stumble, I negotiated my way along a stone wall and out the exit into what had become a magnificent autumn scene.

We walked upon a yellow carpet of caren leaves from trees that stretched from high on a hill to our left to deep in a canyon to our right. And with the sun peeking through at several intervals, it seemed natural to unwrap our basket of pears, bread, cheese and apples and have a picnic, as others were already doing.

This, after all, was part of the Romanian Sunday, too, a chance to savor an afternoon of color and softness in high places, far above the harder and less certain life below — an outlook, the young people believed, that few outsiders could truly appreciate.

Later, at Faget, the day would reveal another mood. There, the sky matched the gray and white station, its three windows each dressed with a box of red flowers, a woman and little girl peering over one of the decorations as the travelers approached the tracks.

Beyond the station, a woman in a purple apron was rounding up geese that had strayed from a pen while, across the road, a gray-haired man in dark, wool trousers and a blue jacket was chasing three cows that were blocking the path of a black Dacia.

The students, meanwhile, were waiting for the train. Most wore jeans. Many wore black, leather jackets or shirts with insignias — Toronto Hockey Club, Jack Daniels, Golden American. Several wore earphones to help them tune in concerts of their own.

On the train, there was no place to sit, the Romanesti returnees joining those already on board in the aisles or between cars on the ride to Timisoara.

As the passengers neared the tan blockhouse at Margina, a light rain was falling and, when the train stopped, a man boarded with a bicycle, even as riders protested that there was no room.

With the windows open and the train easing through open spaces beyond Manastur, the late afternoon was a quiet time, still enough for those near the windows to hear the clang of an oxen bell in a distant pasture and the squeak of black and white guard poles that lifted when the train clattered by.

Like the riders and the train, peasants and wagons were headed home, too, creating occasional silhouettes on hills that stretched toward the horizon.

Further on, with no lights in the train, the car was dark. Old women shared their seats with children. The man with the bicycle departed at Jabar, to be replaced by a woman carrying a duck in a basket.

When the train reached the Timisoara station, the passengers headed for crowded trams. By now, the end had come to a long day, a day of the old and the new, both inside and out.

And as the travelers scattered, Ramona walked to her office where she would write a review with a headline that accurately described the adventure at Pestera Romanesti: "A Happy Time in a Cozy Cave."

A brass band leads
a comeback

Bulgarus. Maryanne Wolf and her friends
returned home one Sunday to give this
village something it had lost — a story

———————————□———————————

"The past has started to fade," she said, having reached the spot where she had lived 20 years before. "There is no one left to tell the story, how things were, how things were done."

It is not as if villagers have stopped talking.

As a busload of visitors arrived at the St. Mary's Catholic Church, in fact, two men chatted beside a horse and wagon, more intent upon their own words and ways than upon those bringing ceremony to the town.

But when Romanians of German descent were allowed to depart the country late in the Ceaucescu regime, many did just that, carrying families and traditions with them, trimming the population of places like Bulgarus by at least half.

Among their rituals was the "kirwei," a celebration of singing, dancing, feasting and prayer marked in Catholic churches each summer, beginning with a mass and lasting for hours, if not longer.

"In the old times, the rejoicing might go for days," Wolf said. "Catholic or not, everyone wanted to take part."

"If you lived here, you belonged."

By 1985, with German families sparse, the kirwei had dwindled to a miniature version of those earlier rites.

"It had been natural for people to know the old ways and teach them to everyone else," Wolf said.

"Years ago, it was easy to find thirty-five couples to dance, all from the village. Now, you may find three or four. And we knew how to make music, too."

When the next August arrived, the kirwei had disappeared and, for nine years, was viewed only as a colorful, and closed, chapter in the two-century history of the church.

If the festival was to come alive, though, it would do so not as an abandoned relic of a nearly-forgotten past, but as a bright and lively being of the present, complete with distinguished guests, imported dancers and a borrowed brass band.

That is how the celebration began to reappear on Sunday morning in Bulgarus, not all at once, but slowly, piece by piece, as one might expect after nearly a decade of slumber.

A German dance troupe from Timisoara piled out of a bus, a tuba player from the village of Recas lugged a brown instrument case toward the school, and two boys from the town of Jebel carried a suitcase stuffed with black vests bearing brass buttons.

This observance, after all, while belonging to Bulgarus, was really a gift from the outside, from dancers and musicians across the Banat region who sought to fan a common, if flickering, heritage in their own special corner of Romania.

And as the guests arrived, they were greeted by parishioners and by curious villagers who watched as the kirwei ingredients began to create the proper mix.

Onlookers also gathered in the churchyard, or beyond its gate, as the mass began, the reds, blues and yellows of the flowers on the altar contrasting with the grayness of the outdoors.

When the mass ended, the parade stepped off, a village march led by the music makers from Recas and featuring 10 couples in vivid kirwei attire.

It was a colorful procession with the members of the 12-piece band, clad in blue and red with plenty of shiny buttons, stepping smartly, two abreast, down brick sidewalks between houses and cherry trees and across streets that had attracted children, many imitating the marchers' rhythmic motions.

The couples who followed the tubas, saxophones, trumpets and baritones wore uniforms as well: the young men in black trousers with black vests over white shirts, and hats topped by heaps of flowers; and the young women in long, white dresses with floral designs.

Later on, those couples danced to waltzes in the school courtyard, and the band leader signaled for the audience to join in.

Soon, the red-brick dance floor was filled, covered with sunshine as well as the laughter and melodies of the kirwei.

This was a time to be treasured, displaying a mood, a verve unfelt in Bulgarus for far too long.

"This is a proud occasion," Uwe Zorn, director of the German consulate in Timisoara, said, amid a dinner of sausage and beer later in the afternoon.

"Our customs have made us strong. We have lived through much upheaval. Now we can smile and celebrate."

Whether a kirwei alone could inspire major changes in a village where life had almost come to a halt might be decided on other, more distant, days.

"Believe it or not," Maryanne Wolf said, "but this community was once teeming with life. Ten stores, instead of a couple. Even a cinema."

During an occasion that prompted fond memories, it was easy for Wolf to remember the days before she left Bulgarus, after high school, for a job in Timisoara.

It was easy, too, even in the glow of the celebration, to see the deserted houses and impassable side streets and wonder what the future might hold.

Still, the afternoon was bright, and Maryanne Wolf was home. The kirwei would last another hour and would return, perhaps, in another year.

"Everything looks better when the sun is shining," she said, watching as sheep crossed the road not far from the dinner and dancing.

And on a day dedicated to a new start in an old place, the presence of the sun was something to be thankful for — that and the pride to be taken in a story well told.

A high and scenic standstill

Anina. With its cargo of logs, kids and card players
in place, the train pulled slowly from the Oravita
station and headed for Anina

—————————☐—————————

The trip would be short, or long, or both, depending upon one's
purpose and point of view.

The town of Anina, in fact, was only 18 miles away, a climb
through the forests of the Anina mountains, then down, with no
scheduled stops in between.

But even though the journey would take an hour and a half, or so
the schedule had stated, time had no meaning to me.

For this was the scenic route, the only daily passenger run on
Romania's oldest line, active since 1864, a road more accustomed to
freight.

This jaunt, too, held reminders of the usual mission: a car stacked
with logs hooked between the engine and the lone passenger car and,
in the riders' compartment, sacks of flour, piled on wooden benches
up front.

And on benches farther back, a woman in a dark bandanna, girl
leaning on her shoulder, was framed by the oval window in the door
that divided the car.

The train swayed as it strained up the mountainside, then, about
halfway there, stopped to take on two railroad workers, hammers in
hand, who had waited by the side of the tracks.

Once on board, the laborers, clad in blue and white overalls, joined
a man in a Honk Kong Drinking Team T-shirt and his partner who had
stretched a board across the seats and had started playing cards before
leaving Oravita.

Outside, meanwhile, the scene was ever-changing, shifting from the dark shade beneath the evergreens to the sun-splashed grandeur of a deep and narrow gorge, then back again.

When the train reached the summit, it slowed and stopped once more, this time without a worker in sight.

Five minutes passed. Then the engine went silent.

A boy grew restless and scrambled over seats. Some passengers peered out windows. Others left the car and walked toward the engine.

We were in a clearing, a flat space among rocks and trees with a station — looking to be the size of a large closet, though probably a little bigger —about 100 yards away.

Soon the message was out that, due to a derailment near Anina, the train would be halted two hours.

I took the news well, wondering what better place to spend any summer afternoon than in the grip of the Anina mountains.

By now, the train was part of the landscape, an iron intruder with dents and scratches on its faded, blue sides accentuated by the June sunshine.

The other passengers, for whom the trek was just a way to reach home, may not have shared my view, but several made the most of the holdup by walking the tracks or sunning themselves on the embankment.

Two boys jumped off the train's high steps, then played tag beside the wheels, even as a woman yelled from above that they be careful.

A Gypsy rested on the grass with her teen-age son and daughter, with the young man urging me to take a picture.

After I did, he pointed down the tracks, perhaps a quarter of a mile, and at the man coming toward us with a bottle of water in each hand.

I walked that way and reached a spring where cool water flowed from a natural fountain among the rocks.

As I cupped my hands and began to drink, the bubbling almost obscured another sound, the horn of the train.

In the distance, one of the boys signaled, and, as I started to run, the blare from the diesel continued, a sign to pick up the pace.

When I neared the car, a woman in a polka dot dress and blue scarf was laughing and waving her arms, as if cheering me across a finish line.

After I reached the steps, the train creaked and moved, an hour after the break began.

With that, all was as it had been before: a rail worker shuffling his cards, the mother and daughter still seated behind the oval window, the flour sacks still secure on the seats.

To me, the remaining hour to Anina offered much promise, just as the trip up the mountain had done.

And in Anina, what I had thought would be my real adventure — a weekend hike — would begin.

But while I would measure that journey in miles, I would count the day's memories in moments, with the brightest reserved for a pause on a mountain and a train that could only stand still.

yellow

yellow

yellow

yellow

The journey told a story

Virfurile. Transylvania

―――――― □ ――――――

The shortest day of the year.

The train will continue to Brad — Romanian for "Christmas tree" — but I depart at the village of Virfurile amid a soft rain and the scent of evergreen.

Christmas is, in fact, only four days away, and the trees on the gentle slopes of the Apuseni mountains give flavor to the season, add color to the otherwise gray landscape of a late-December morning.

The setting speaks of holidays, but the story is not so simple. For in Romania, seasons are not always as they seem, and, even in this tranquil place, the ancient celebration must blend with a modern remembrance, the revolution of 1989.

The observances do not so much blend as collide, the revolution providing its own sense of darkness, light and mystery that forever haunts Romanian life, especially in December.

For Sabin Mihit, though, the day's first chore is clear. And as I approach his backyard, to the accompaniment of barking dogs, he and his neighbor are slaughtering a pig that will supply food for months to come.

"We must live off our animals," Mihit said, having stored the pork in a shed behind his house.

"Life in a village moves very, very slowly. Change is something we hear about but cannot see."

Across the lane, meanwhile, George Crainic savors hot tea beside a wood stove, recalling the day he learned that change can simply mean finding the courage to lift a finger.

Crainic was in Timisoara on Dec. 16 when the uprising began. It would spread to other cities the next day and lead to the downfall of dictator Nicolae Ceausescu a week later.

"I met my high school daughter at the train station," he said, "and I heard shots in the distance."

"A man shouted: 'It's starting. We'll soon be free.' I stood for a minute, then thought of what to do."

To Crainic, that meant scrawling "Jos (Down With) Ceausescu" with his finger on the sides of his dust-caked van, a message he carried, to the tune of a honking horn, through Galsa, Misca and Pincota on the five-hour ride back to Virfurile.

"When I slowed down, people yelled: 'No, no. You cannot say that.' But I replied that it is true. Our suffering is ending."

As Crainic speaks, a horse and wagon pass by the window and, next door, his mother, Lenuta, and wife, Carolina, are arranging for another journey to Timisoara.

During Ceausescu's regime, Dec. 25 was an ordinary work day, and persons who displayed trees explained, if asked, that they were only marking a moment in Romanian history or the coming of the new year.

But that, too, has changed.

The next morning, two hours before sunrise, as lightbulbs strung on a wire flicker in a mist, George, Lenuta and Carolina Crainic finish the work begun the day before, of loading all the Christmas trees that will fit into the trailer behind a small truck for delivery to Timisoara and points along the way.

To the family, the venture has become a tradition all its own.

"I have my customers every year," George said. "I give them the best I can find and cut, the best from Virfurile."

When all is ready, I take my place on a narrow bench in the windowless rear of the truck with Carolina and four villagers who will ride to Arad, a city of 200,000, four hours away.

The inside is dark, the road bumpy, the truck grinds and strains from pulling its weighty cargo.

For me, this is an adventure, but I am curious what the Romanians are thinking on this Dec. 22, the national holiday of the revolution, the anniversary of the day the Ceausescus fled from Bucharest by helicopter, following 24 years in power.

I find the answer moments later when George begins to sing and is quickly joined by the others. The song, "O Ce Veste Minunata (O What Wonderful News)," is a carol sung so frequently in recent Decembers that it is practically considered a national hymn.

The song ends, but the trek continues, through Seleus, Ineu and Aldesti. Then, as the truck slows, I hear a thumping on the door. We are at a stoplight in Arad and, on this gray morning, a white-haired man in a brown suit and overcoat has spotted our freight.

Traffic swerves around the truck while George and his customer negotiate the price of a tree. Moments later, the man hands over 2,000 lei (about $1.20), pulls an evergreen from the trailer and, tree in one arm, red briefcase in the other, disappears around the nearest corner.

Within an hour after the Crainics arrive in Timisoara, the trees are gone, deposited with sellers in market lots or sold to others who stopped the truck, just as the man in Arad had done.

But Christmas is still three days away, and more trees await in Virfurile.

So, as the revolution is marked in Timisoara, George Crainic is going home, only to return the next day, only to meet still another mission, with still another message, along the roads he travels in December.

Partners in clippers and yarn

Vinga. The man and woman were busy — he with his clippers, she with her yarn

---

I tried not to disturb them, but, when they saw me, they worked even harder, proud of their effort and their craft.

They toiled by the roadside, 100 miles apart, unknown to each other, performing tasks that were not the same.

But their labors blended, at least in my thoughts, after travels on two afternoons.

I saw him south of Vinga, among the trees, surrounded by sheep, wool and two young men who packed their harvest into burlap bags.

Cars and trucks cruised the two-lane highway between Timisoara and Arad, and, now and then, one pulled into a restaurant parking lot in view of the men and the sheep.

The workers barely noticed the traffic and, when the time came, their shady grove near a bend in the road would be rest stop enough for them.

By the time I approached, the young men had flung the sacks over their shoulders and were hauling them toward a wagon.

The other man, meanwhile, had one arm around a sheep's neck and was shearing the animal with the other.

Although intent in his chore, the man turned the sheep toward me, then smiled, as if approving of my interest by granting a much closer look.

He worked quickly, gently and in partnership with the sheep as the clicking of shears occasionally mixed with the hum of a passing car.

Staring in my direction, in fact, the animal appeared more uneasy about my intention than with the upcoming loss of its coat.

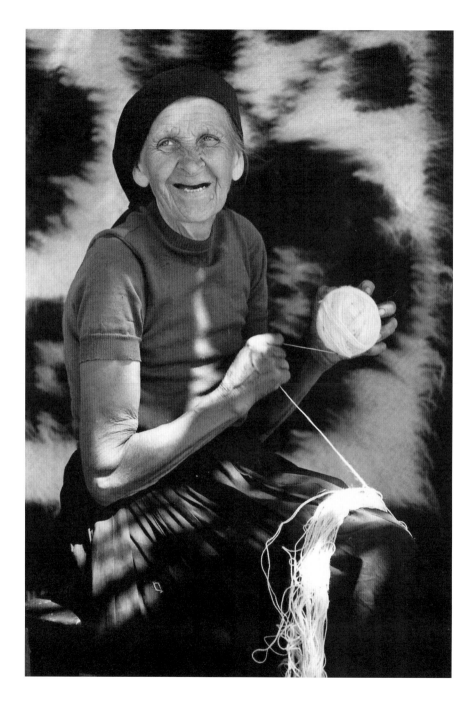

The man, whose lined face and tan complexion attested to many warm days in the fields, was following an old tradition, though his blue beret and digital watch rendered a decidedly modern touch.

And when he finished adding another layer to the wool carpet beneath the oaks, he released the sheep, nodded and hesitated a moment, like an actor awaiting applause.

I did not cheer, but offered a handshake, receiving, in return, the same from the man and his young companions.

The ritual in wool would be performed many more times that day by the men near Vinga and by many other shepherds in many other Romanian fields.

And while those locations might include Sapinta, south of the Ukrainian border, I changed focus while visiting there a week later.

This time, the woman with her yarn appeared, creating, in an instant, a summer scene that differed from the one in Vinga.

She was seated on a wooden box near the village square, a white, woolen blanket with red and black designs behind her, wresting not with a cumbersome sheep but with endless strands of twisted fibers which she tamed with devotion and dexterity.

After a facile journey through her fingers, the string would add to a growing ball of yarn which, later on, would wend its way to her worn but reliable loom, there to become one more line in a statement of brightness and style.

Nestled in the mountains of Maramures, with an historic church and cemetery at its center, Sapinta draws more visitors than the ordinary Romanian village, though, by most measures, it could not be called a tourist town.

And after decades of turning hard work into art work, much of it through the same loom she now employed, the woman was not likely to change her ways, whatever the size of her audience.

The long, white yarn, a contrast to her dark clothes, picked up speed as I stood by. Then the weaver urged me to handle the large blanket, a gesture she made partly for sale, but partly for pride as well.

In the end, after all, the man in Vinga and the woman in Sapinta did belong to the same slice of memory, if not to the same afternoon.

If their ways were quaint, at least in a world wed to efficiency, their lessons in wool were ones worth learning.

For they treated their duties with ease, purpose and cheer, as if masking the skills it took to perform them.

And it was the display of those traits, unscripted and with a texture and hue equal to any blanket on any Romanian roadside, that provided the most lasting souvenir of all.

A message for a stranger

Berzovia. The boys and girls sat quietly, engrossed by
the woman who read to them beneath the oak tree

———————□———————

She smiled, frowned, told stories, then, scanning the circle, coaxed
her listeners to tell tales of their own.

The woman read not from a book but from a well-worn deck of
cards whose simple words and pictures, in the hands of a skillful
interpreter, might address deep-running currents in the provinces of
destiny and chance.

The reader was Adriana, a Gypsy, and it seemed those provinces,
even without the direction of tarot cards, had guided me to a fortune
of pleasant moments on that summer day.

I had seen Gypsies in Timisoara, often begging or selling cups of
sunflower seeds near the football stadium or in the city center.

And, in my own way, I wanted to learn more about them, without
really knowing how.

The opportunity came in Berzovia where, for a time, I was the
gypsy, one who stopped wandering when spotted by Adriana, a sign
of hospitality and a reminder that curiosity works best when shared.

Berzovia, a farming village, is best known as a station to change
trains enroute to Oravita, Resita and Timisoara.

When that happens, the rail platform becomes the busiest place in
town, where passengers scurry between cars, vendors hawk candy at
windows to buyers with outstretched hands, and the ensuing clamor
outdoes any noise ever heard on Berzovia's streets.

As I walked along those streets, in fact, the sounds were confined
to roosters, tractors and the creaking chain which carried the bucket
of water that I pulled from a well.

The water was the perfect tonic for a day that threatened to be the hottest of the summer, a time better suited to staying still than walking around.

Then I noticed a man on a bench, or perhaps he noticed me.

He was leaning against an orange-brick house and, as he started to wave, a woman in a window called me over.

And suddenly, a couple steps later, I was in the middle of a family or a neighborhood, or a little of both.

It would take a while to figure out where each parent, grandparent, friend and child belonged, but I was in no hurry.

For the kids and dogs and those who watched over them seemed to be in just the right place, though distracted by the visitor who had drifted into their yard.

There was Adriana, a dark-skinned woman with a gold dress, white blouse with bright, red and blue dots and a heart-shaped tattoo marked "Sam" on her arm who introduced me to everyone in sight.

And Constantin Nelu, a young man who would invite me for dinner with his wife, Rodica, and daughter, Daniela, 7, in their house across the road.

And the children, a dozen in all and in virtually all sizes, whom I would accompany to a swimming hole on the other side of town.

The swimming trip began as a long and orderly line, with the children — the boys brandishing water pistols — trooping behind Constantin, yelling to a man watching from a wagon and scaring some geese as they went.

Once there, they splashed below a dam, beside others who were also relishing the August afternoon.

In a way, this was an instant that might have been captured anywhere, but this was a day in Romania.

And as I sat on a blanket drinking tea with Constantin, his wife, parents, grandmother and an assortment of friends, I was reminded that I was not merely outside the circle of children who listened to Adriana.

I was also far from the center of the culture whose borders I had been invited to touch.

The reminder had been my own, for the hosts had made me feel at home with the tea and warm bread and by providing the most comfortable corner of the blanket.

For now, at least, we were pleased simply by what we could share — brief companionship — and what little I could offer: answers to questions about who I am and where I came from; milk and a bottle of wine; and a promise to send pictures of the children, snapped in the brief intervals when the youngest were not pushing their eyes against the lens.

When it was time to leave, Adriana reached into her cards and, smiling at the selection, showed me one. The card contained a black and white silhouette of a man and woman holding hands. A corner read "Dragoste" (Love).

After that, four of the men escorted me to the depot through a field, along a paved road, then down the dusty streets of a Gypsy settlement.

It was twilight, and everything had a tint of gold whether a goat nibbling grass, a girl standing on a bench between trees or people sitting in doorways or dipping buckets into a stone well.

As we continued on, the pace quickened, the train only minutes away.

But as I walked, I collected images, passing glimpses of people I may never see again who, in these final moments in Berzovia, flashed by in portraits more telling than any of my pictures might reveal.

This had really been a day of images from the start, of studied glances and exchanged reflections in color and black and white, whether exposed by card or camera.

And if their value was not clear, it was sufficient merely to have made them, to savor my final steps through the village and to ponder the deeper meaning much later, if at all.

Night train to the Rose Bowl

Aboard the Rapid 12. Three passengers and
a conductor pressed toward the window, even
though there was little to see

———————□———————

For they were not seeking to approach the blackness of a summer
night but a small, red radio that would link the train to a happening
on the other side of the world.

The destination was Bucharest but, in a sense, it was also the Rose
Bowl, where the Romanian soccer team was taking on Argentina in
the World Cup.

The blond woman holding the radio cursed softly as she sought
the place where static would give way to an announcer's voice and
the report that the entire country was waiting to hear.

And when the signal emerged from the noise, it had to compete,
as it would all night, with the jouncing of the train against the rails
and the sound of the wind as it roared past open windows elsewhere
in the sleeping car.

Although the sight of soccer fans stuffed in an aisle at midnight
could have seemed unusual, it did not faze a gray-haired Swedish
traveler who, clad in a blue robe, left his compartment to see what
the fuss was about.

"I recall taking a train through Germany during 1954 when the
Germans were playing Hungary in the finals," he said, sliding along
the smutty floor in his white slippers.

"All the towns were in an uproar. As I remember, the trainman
didn't bother to collect the fare."

The conductor on the Bucharest run, however, had not been so
careless, starting his rounds moments after 11 o'clock when the
train left Timisoara on its eight-hour journey.

And he was careful to leave his red and blue, wool jacket, brass buttons and black necktie intact, even in a place whose sweltering atmosphere assured the fans of having something in common with the spectators in Pasadena where the temperature was nearing 100 degrees.

I listened in the aisle, too, waiting for my companions to decipher the scratchy reception into something I could understand.

Their response, when it came, was universal, an outburst of cheers followed by a "Hai Romania" chant after the Romanians had scored the first goal. One of the listeners, a middle-aged man with plaid shirt and black moustache, tossed his cigarette into the air, and the woman shook the radio above her head, prompting another temporary loss of the signal.

When the goal was scored, I was leaning out the window as we glided into Lugoj, beside a silent station dressed in gold and black tiles where a railroad worker slowly swung a green lantern at the passing train.

Somewhere beyond that station, horns honked and shouts broke out, just as the eruption was occurring in the sleeper.

It was a national moment of joy, but, like all moments, it had to end, this one with a goal by Argentina.

"You are soccer players, not tourists," the blond woman snapped, as her colleagues nodded in agreement.

"Do not embarrass us before the world."

But as the train pressed on, so did the Romanian soccer team, adding another goal before halftime — or maybe two.

With Romania leading 2-1, the fans cheered again, before being told by a conductor that they had misheard the announcer and that a goal had not been scored.

Amid the confusion, the Swedish traveler, observing from his doorway, decided to retire, shutting his door after saying:

"I'm so sorry, but I don't understand any of this."

I spent the halftime break sitting on my top berth, window wide open, letting the air rush by, knowing that, because of the heat and the game, I would do little sleeping the rest of the night.

As I sat there, faint specks of light often broke the darkness, perhaps Jupa or Costeiu or Topolovatu or one of the many other little places enroute to the nation's largest city.

And though I could not see those villages, I felt certain the people there were watching or listening to the game, just as I had done with friends in Timisoara when Romania had played Colombia and Switzerland.

The World Cup had, in fact, arrived in Timisoara in ways both large and small, from the appearance of a 30-foot inflatable soccer ball, bearing Coca-Cola emblems, in Opera Square to the sale of "American World Cup Popcorn" and stickers featuring stars Dan Petrescu and Gheorghe Popescu and superstar Gheorghe Hagi.

And Ovidiu Forai, a sportswriter for the newspaper Timisoara, had predicted that the World Cup, as usual, would be much more than a sporting event.

"The first mission of sports is to make people know each other better," he said.

"We have a very high sense of how people see us, how they see all Romanians. And, most especially, how the United States views Romanians."

If that purpose seemed too ambitious to be met on a world scale in one day, it was at least being honored in the sleeping car aisle where a young man in a white T-shirt and blue pajama bottoms, who had been following the action all night, instructed the conductor to bring beer to the fans standing by the window as the second half began.

The trainman quickly complied, retreating into a compartment containing a refrigerator marked "Defect" (Out of Order) and returning with four bottles of warm "Timisoara."

When uncapped, the bottles oozed with foam, inspiring less than a champagne toast but building a moment that, like the one the Swede had remembered from 40 years before, no one would be likely to forget.

The observance, in fact, came in anticipation of a victory, not following the win itself. That would come later, after Romania had added a goal and Argentina had retaliated to make the final score 3-2.

After the game, I stayed in the aisle a little longer, still looking for those tiny towns I could not see, imagining how, the next day, children would chase soccer balls along dusty streets or in open fields, pretending to be Petrescu or Hagi.

That fantasy would be shared by those in the nation's capital, too, a place where a celebration of the triumph had sent people to the streets in numbers that rivaled the days of the revolution.

For upon arriving in Bucharest, it was easy to feel that there was something special in the air, something other than the heat and the dirt that was already promising another oppressive summer day.

The huge front-page headline of the newspaper Libertatea said it best: "Victorie!"

And whether expressed by the half-million, in the streets of Bucharest, or by the handful, in the aisle of a train, the message was clear to all: it had been a great night to be Romanian, even if no one else was watching.

A bishop and a birthday

Belint. Priest Tarziu Constantin stood before
the Sunday gathering, raised his hand and
awaited the proper response

---□---

It came a moment later just as he had hoped: the sounds of a clarinet, a saxophone and an electric guitar, the cue for the Rev. Constantin to join in.

With that, he sang the first of many folk tunes to the 200 people who had come to the Belint village school to celebrate.

The song told of a man who had left his village but had always remembered the place and its people, a perfect theme for Belint's 625th birthday party.

For a town that traced its beginnings to 1369, during the reign of Hungarian King Ludovic I, a single day might have seemed little time to commemorate all that had gone before.

But on that bright Sunday, the villagers had decided to try, posting a welcoming committee at the train station or, for one visitor, along the highway that runs through Belint.

That special guest was Nicolae Corneanu, Orthodox bishop of metropolitan Timisoara, who had journeyed 30 miles by car, then stepped into a carriage pulled by two flower-bedecked horses.

The buggy, modeled after royal carriages of the Austro-Hungarian empire, lent majesty to his arrival, as women in blue and gold peasant costumes locked arms beside the road and children waved at the man with white beard and black robe who rode above flowery wheels which spun red and yellow.

The focus of the celebration was the Belint Orthodox Church, built in 1798 and, in many ways, the center of community life.

The church, in fact, rests on the public square, a few footsteps from the village well where people would later line up to fetch cool water.

A monument in the churchyard, a tall cross atop a stone base, honors, in a personal way, 38 Belint men killed in service during World War I. In addition to listing names, the memorial records addresses: "Prohab Ion 422" or "Marcu Dimilrie 888."

Several boys sat on that monument, others in trees, hoping for a closer look at the bishop as his carriage passed the well, scattering dust as it approached the church gate.

By then, the entire congregation had gathered in the street, beside the fence and in the yard. Three boys watched from a second-story window, the green, open shutters set against the white walls of the church.

Women in scarves, symbols of marriage, stood next to girls wearing white dresses with intricate red and blue patterns on the sleeves.

When the carriage reached the gate, a red and gray carpet was there, too, unfurled by two boys in black trousers and white shirts who waited at the walkway, almost as if standing at attention until Bishop Nicolae had passed.

The church crowded, many worshipers knelt outside where the bishop's words were transmitted through a loudspeaker tied to a tree.

While many listened, though, others were at work.

Men sliced freshly-baked bread and pastries on tables behind the church while women placed cakes and pies on tables in front.

After mass, the bishop would bless the colorful array of treats, most bearing cross-shaped insignias, and share the bounty with everyone.

The main meal of the day — the "festival dinner" — would be served in the afternoon at the school.

I walked there down the broad, main street which, at this special time, was both playground and flea market.

A boy, still in the blue shirt he had worn to church, blew up balloons in the square while a girl in a flowery dress enjoyed an ice cream cone.

Others shopped at tables where sellers offered cigarettes, sun glasses, "Beverly Hills 90210" cards or Turbo gum. Plastic earrings and plastic watches dangled from strings, and Pepsi-Colas rested in tubs of ice.

Earlier, a member of the organizing committee had said that the observance was not so much a commemoration of a single event but of deeds done by ordinary villagers — farmers, teachers, soldiers, parents — over more than six centuries that had helped Belint survive.

"Every day is different," he said, "like anyplace else."

"We work with patience, the best we can."

The village, while still home to many farmers, is a commuter town, too, with residents who drive to jobs in Timisoara.

"And our young people used to stay home every night," the man added. "Now they go to discos."

At the school, meanwhile, the feast was underway with diners seated in the main hall, in classrooms and in hallways.

Despite the squeeze, there was room enough, and food enough, for all.

Meats, milk, fruits and vegetables — products of the fields of Belint — packed the tables. Women carrying large bowls of potatoes or heaping plates of eggplant or cabbage eked through narrow rows of chairs to serve the crowd.

Rev. Constantin and his trio sat in a corner, having space for their instruments and an amplifier, and not much more.

To the priest, returning home, from Paris, held a bittersweet quality.

For it was his first visit to Belint since the revolution, and since the death of his father.

"Many here today and those who came before us have known much pain here," he said, "but they have given us much good, much to build on."

He recalled his own days in the 220-year-old school, thanking the teachers and referring to pictures on the wall showing long tables in those same halls where children were fed during times of war.

"Now we have some hope," he said. "With all the difficulties of our present and our past, we can see a happy future."

Then the Rev. Tarziu Constantin shed a tear.

Then he sang another song.

Rhythm with a view

Petrosanti. The train trip through
the mountains had it all

———————□———————

Scenery, companions — and a surprise in a big, plastic bag.

And when it was over, I was reminded that even the longest ride sometimes ends too soon.

The day was brilliant, the countryside in bloom.

It was an experience to be savored and, best of all, to be shared — if only with strangers whose sole bond was their common destination.

A round-faced woman in a brown scarf, green sweater and blue socks sat by the window holding the plastic bag.

A boy in a red, knit bonnet with white stripes stared across from me while his father dozed.

A man in a brown suit and off-white sweater leaned his head against a pillow as a tan case rested on his lap.

And the couple next to me, each dressed in shiny black — she with her spidery stockings, he with his gold, chain necklace — browsed through the Morbida Fascinatie (Fascinating Death) newspaper.

In the aisle, meanwhile, a man in a blue beret lowered the window and looked out, between puffs on his Carpati cigarettes.

We were travelers on a journey to Bucharest, about eight hours from Cluj-Napoca, where the run had started, and six hours from the village of Hateg, where I had boarded with three others.

A trip of that duration requires planning, as each rider in our Wagon 10 compartment seemed to know.

As proof, sacks stuffed with apples, pears, cans of water, breads and jams appeared now and then in answer to the meager, and expensive, food on board.

And, as the minutes passed, the woman in black pulled a deck of worn playing cards, with a sunflower design on the back, from her purse and dealt a hand to her neighbor and the man in the brown suit.

The boy, meanwhile, had taken off his shoes and gazed at his father who was removing a banana from a paper sack.

At the same time, the woman by the window reached into the plastic bag, pushed a button and settled back.

With that, red and green lights flashed from within, and, after that, music filled the compartment.

Whether intentional or not, the blinking cassette player would provide accompaniment for the scene outside the train, a view that had prompted the players to turn away from their cards and the boy and his dad to look out the window.

For the southern Carpathian mountains were now at their spring best, displaying roads that stretched to the sky and craggy hillsides dressed with gray spots of sheep.

Later on, a rock fence crossed rows of trees sporting frilly, white blossoms, and the land abounded in giant splashes of undulating green.

Once in a while, an orange, tiled roof emerged on the horizon, the kind that rises above a porch with colorful carpets and a wayward rooster or two.

It seemed, in fact, as if everything was swarming gently over itself in a cadence that matched the music in the plastic bag.

That music — an accordian, a clarinet, a "pipes over squeeze box" sound — was rhythmic and gentle with almost a lullaby effect. And, in the woman's hands, the player was a gift, muted just right, as if meant to entertain each passenger.

Maybe it is too much to believe that sounds on tape and the off-beat clatter of wheels on rails could cast a spell.

But that is how it seemed, if only for a while, as the passengers, enthralled, watched the world come alive, the Carpathians and their people renew themselves, as they had for centuries.

It was a setting observed from a distance, without the intrusion of politics and economics. And, if that train window provided a simple look at life, it was a glimpse that offered the viewers a few

undeniable certainties: that the land was vibrant, strong, beautiful — and belonged to them.

Further along, as the train passed over the narrow, tumultuous rapids of the Jiu River, a vendor, dressed in a white jacket, opened the compartment door and took orders for coffee.

After pouring the coffee into cups set on a brass tray, he closed the door, just as the train had entered a tunnel.

As the train moved on, the cassette player still blinked green and red in the dark while the music played.

On the other side, the landscape was green again — but not for long.

For soon, the far-off houses with bright roofs had given way to soot-stained dwellings near the tracks, homes of brick and wood.

Near the station, a man in a red and orange jacket pushed a trash cart along a narrow street, and a rail gang in gray hammered track in an adjacent freight yard.

This was Petrosanti, a gritty, coal town of 50,000, where the train would make a 10-minute stop.

During that pause, new passengers pushed suitcases and duffel bags along the narrow aisle, having boarded for trips to Craiova or beyond.

There would be time enough to buy sandwiches through the open windows or for a boy to run from the train and drink from the blackened, concrete fountain next to the depot.

Arrival at Petrosanti was a reminder that the trip through the mountains had ended and that a three-hour ride on the plain to Bucharest lay ahead.

The most colorful part of the journey was over, the one that seemed a perfect mix of sun, sky, land and people, set to the music of a cassette player that no one saw.

But this was Romania, too, and, whether through green or grime, a spring train ride was presenting the country in a variety of shades, each gliding by under a blue sky.

So the woman in the spidery stockings dealt five more cards to the man in the brown suit as the cassette player continued to twinkle and pipe.

And, moments later, the train was gone again.

Flowers, pizza, the people down the street

I called them "neighbors"

We lived in Timisoara where Sportivilor and December 1 streets come together and trams numbered 3, 6 and 9 rattle among towering, concrete apartment blocks of scrubby orange and gray.

The neighborhood has a weary look that might even be called dreary, especially when the fog rolls in during late autumn and sticks around through most of the winter.

But color is where you find it, and, at times, it depends upon who is looking.

"You're a strange person around here," a friend told me, pointing out that I was the first American ever to have lived in or near Block 88 A on December 1.

And if residents wondered about the tall man who walked their streets, often with a basketball under his arm, I wondered, too, about this tiny piece of Romania that, for a year, was home.

When color came to the neighborhood — at least to my eyes — it did so in specks instead of splashes, as if slowly painting a picture in which I finally felt that I belonged.

The red, plastic scoop by the popcorn machine where customers lined up on cool, fall evenings, their faces aglow from the bulb that dangled inside. The gold beret of the carrot seller who set up shop each day beside his wooden crate, then retired to his "chair," a tree stump. The green graffiti ("Paradise Lost" and "Don't Loose Ya Brain") sprayed on a wall behind a grocery store.

What brought the neighborhood into sharpest focus, though, were the people who lived there.

I saw them in the apartment blocks and on the streets, not so absorbed with color or focus but with nothing more than going about their lives.

I remember their faces and many of their names, and, in a given moment, can assemble a random patchwork of those figures that remain most vivid.

* An electrician in a fourth-floor flat on Sportivilor. A board member of the Reformed Church of Timisoara, he backed the Rev. Laszlo Tokes in the days preceding the revolution, despite threats to his family.

* Dorel and Lia Jurcovan, in a sixth-floor flat near the tram line. They opened one of Timisoara's first pizza parlors and direct other businesses from an office on the former Karl Marx Street.

* Johnell Spitarro, a hydraulic engineer, who scored 14 points against a touring NBA all-star team in May 1 Stadium, at the end of Sportivilor, on a rainy afternoon in 1965. "Spini" showed me a medallion commemorating that game, adding that "in sports, all people are the same."

* The family in the apartment below me. The mother is a teacher, the father a merchant sailor, the daughter a University of Timisoara freshman, studying law. When I left Timisoara, they gave me a 100 lei coin with the likeness of King Mihai dated 1946, the year before the family farm in a nearby village was confiscated.

* The people who appeared each morning to sell eggs, flowers, ice cream, bananas, Snickers bars, grapes, peppers, melons, cat tails or whatever else was available that day.

* The retired Army doctor who liked American movies and Broadway shows. I enjoyed a nine-hour Christmas dinner with his family, and, a short while later, I was invited back to watch the film "Yankee Doodle Dandy" on TV.

* The man on a side street who filled his horse-drawn wagon with grass cut by hand on the university grounds. He smiled when I passed by and patted his gray horse, as if acknowledging the reason I took a second look.

* The women who swept the streets with brooms made of long branches. The streets held signs directing the way to Bucuresti, Lugoj, Belgrad, Moravita and Resita or touting Apple computers or a "Trash Metal Attack" concert.

The scenes, the contrasts might take a while for an outsider to fully comprehend.

"We are very exotic, unless you are used to us," a doctor said, as we shared coffee at the Orizont restaurant next to my building.

"Perhaps as unusual to you as an octopus playing a banjo, flying over a stream."

But such a sight would have been far less remarkable than what I really saw.

For these were rather ordinary people who are extraordinary merely for having endured a world which I could view only in distant glances.

Not so long ago, for example, the neighborhood at Sportivilor and December 1 would have been a much darker place to visit.

That is when Romanians were forbidden to speak to foreigners and were spied upon by security forces and when, by government action, electricity was turned off most of the day.

No bananas were sold on the streets back then. Most children had never even seen one before.

But those who outlasted the worst of days do not see themselves as heroes, nor do I.

For they are not statues in a park nor do they wear uniforms with medals.

If you go to Timisoara, you can still see them where Sportivilor meets December 1.

I just called them "neighbors."

red

red

red

red